JOSH STEVE

The Audit Anomaly

Copyright © 2023 by Josh Steve

All rights reserved. No part of this publication may be reproduced, stored or transmitted in any form or by any means, electronic, mechanical, photocopying, recording, scanning, or otherwise without written permission from the publisher. It is illegal to copy this book, post it to a website, or distribute it by any other means without permission.

This novel is entirely a work of fiction. The names, characters and incidents portrayed in it are the work of the author's imagination. Any resemblance to actual persons, living or dead, events or localities is entirely coincidental.

Josh Steve asserts the moral right to be identified as the author of this work.

First edition

*This book was professionally typeset on Reedsy.
Find out more at reedsy.com*

Contents

The Discovery	1
Whispers of Deceit	5
Uncovering Clues	9
The Corporate Cover-Up	13
Partners in Crime	17
A Trail of Destruction	22
The Hunter Becomes the Hunted	26
The Deadly Chase	30
The Testimony	35
The Final Gambit	39
The Showdown	44
Unveiling the Conspiracy	48

The Discovery

The office hummed with the monotonous drone of fluorescent lights. Sarah Walker sat hunched over her cluttered desk, her eyes glued to a spreadsheet that seemed determined to defy her understanding. She had always thrived on unraveling financial puzzles, but this one was different. This one made her stomach churn with unease.

The Financial Integrity Department of Everest Corp was her domain, a place where balance sheets met scrutiny, and anomalies were ruthlessly hunted down. At thirty-five, Sarah had earned a reputation as a financial sleuth with an unerring eye for detail. Her colleagues often teased her about her relentless pursuit of discrepancies, but it was a trait that had made her the best in the business.

Today, however, even her well-honed instincts couldn't prepare her for what she was about to discover.

The numbers on her screen formed a labyrinth of confusion, but there was one line that caught her eye—an anomaly so glaring it might as well have been a neon sign flashing "Investigate Me." It was a simple entry, just one figure on a sprawling spreadsheet of revenue and expenses, but it stood out like a jagged crack in the facade of Everest Corp's financial statements.

THE AUDIT ANOMALY

Sarah couldn't believe her eyes. "Impossible," she muttered under her breath. She reached for her calculator, her fingers trembling ever so slightly as she punched in the numbers. The result confirmed her worst suspicions. Everest Corp, a multi-billion-dollar conglomerate, was reporting a revenue figure that was off by a staggering ten million dollars.

Her heart raced as she contemplated the implications. A discrepancy of this magnitude couldn't be brushed aside as a simple accounting error. It was a red flag waving in the face of Everest Corp's impeccable reputation. A red flag that suggested something nefarious was afoot.

Sarah knew she had to investigate further, but she also understood the gravity of what she was about to undertake. Uncovering financial irregularities in a company of Everest's stature could have far-reaching consequences, both for her career and for the company itself. She had to be absolutely certain before she took the next step.

With a sense of urgency, Sarah began to dig deeper. She pulled up transaction records, combed through invoices, and scrutinized every detail of Everest Corp's financial history. The more she delved into the numbers, the more convinced she became that this was no ordinary mistake.

Hidden within the labyrinth of financial data were signs of deliberate manipulation. Payments to obscure vendors, transactions that seemed to serve no legitimate purpose, and a pattern of expenses that defied logic—all of it pointed to a carefully orchestrated scheme to inflate revenue.

As the hours stretched into the night, Sarah's determination grew stronger. She was no longer driven solely by professional curiosity. She felt a growing sense of responsibility to uncover the truth. Everest Corp was a giant in the corporate world, and if they were engaging in financial misconduct, it could have devastating consequences for investors, employees, and the economy at large.

But Sarah was also acutely aware of the dangers of her pursuit. She had heard stories of auditors who had uncovered corporate fraud and had their lives turned upside down. Whistleblowers who had been silenced, their careers and reputations destroyed. She couldn't afford to be reckless.

She reached for her phone and dialed a number she had saved for emergencies. The voice on the other end was hushed, and Sarah recognized it immediately. It was David, a former colleague who had gone underground after exposing a major corporate scandal years ago.

"David," she whispered urgently, "I need your help. I've stumbled onto something big, something that goes deep within Everest Corp."

There was a pause on the other end of the line, and then David's voice came through, tinged with a mixture of concern and caution. "Sarah, you know what you're getting into, right? These people play dirty. You could be risking everything."

"I know," Sarah replied, her voice unwavering. "But I can't turn a blind eye to this. I need your guidance, your expertise. I don't know who I can trust anymore."

David sighed. "Okay, meet me tomorrow at the usual place. We'll go over everything you've found so far. But remember, Sarah, once you go down this path, there's no turning back."

The call ended, leaving Sarah with a knot of anxiety in her chest. She knew she was stepping onto a treacherous path, one that would test her skills, her integrity, and her courage. But she couldn't walk away from the truth. Not when the very foundations of Everest Corp's financial integrity seemed to be crumbling before her eyes.

As she shut down her computer and gathered her belongings, Sarah couldn't shake the feeling that she was about to embark on the most perilous journey of her career. The discovery of that one glaring anomaly had set in motion a chain of events that would lead her deep into the heart of corporate darkness, where secrets were buried, and deception thrived.

Little did she know that her pursuit of the truth would unearth not only the hidden machinations of Everest Corp but also the depths of her own determination and resilience. The shadows of suspense and intrigue had descended upon her life, and there was no turning back now.

Whispers of Deceit

The sun had dipped below the city skyline, casting long shadows across the bustling streets of Manhattan. Sarah Walker sat in a dimly lit corner of a small, inconspicuous cafe, waiting for David. The aroma of freshly brewed coffee wafted through the air, but she had little appetite. Her mind was consumed by the web of deception she had stumbled upon at Everest Corp.

David arrived, his appearance as unassuming as ever—a man in his forties with salt-and-pepper hair and a face etched with the scars of battles fought in the world of corporate espionage. He slipped into the seat across from Sarah, his eyes scrutinizing her with a mix of concern and curiosity.

"Sarah," he began, his voice low and measured, "tell me everything you've found so far."

She leaned in closer, her voice barely above a whisper. "It's worse than I thought, David. The revenue discrepancy I found—it's not just a simple error. I've traced it back to a pattern of manipulated transactions."

David raised an eyebrow. "Manipulated transactions? Deliberate deception, then."

Sarah nodded. "Yes, and it goes beyond that. I've uncovered a network of shell companies and fictitious vendors. It's like they've been siphoning off money, inflating their revenue for years."

David leaned back, deep in thought. "This is big, Sarah. Everest Corp is a behemoth. If what you're saying is true, it could shake the very foundations of the corporate world."

"I know," Sarah replied, her voice tinged with trepidation. "That's why I called you. I need your expertise. I need to know how deep this goes, and who's behind it."

David took a sip of his coffee, his gaze fixed on Sarah. "First, we need to be cautious. We're dealing with powerful people who won't hesitate to protect their interests. You said you don't know who you can trust anymore—keep it that way for now. Loose lips sink ships, Sarah."

She understood the gravity of his words. Trust had become a rare and precious commodity in her world, and the walls of secrecy were closing in around her.

"David, what's our next move?" Sarah asked, her determination clear.

"We start by gathering more evidence," he replied. "We need irrefutable proof of the fraud. But we also need to remain invisible, off the radar. If Everest Corp catches wind of our investigation, they'll do everything in their power to shut us down."

Over the next few weeks, Sarah and David embarked on a clandestine operation to peel back the layers of deception that shrouded Everest Corp. They communicated through encrypted messages, met in secret locations, and used every trick in the book to stay off the grid.

Sarah's days at the office became a delicate balancing act. On the surface, she continued her routine audits and meetings, all while surreptitiously gathering incriminating evidence. She became a master of concealment, hiding files and documents in encrypted folders and maintaining an impeccable facade of business as usual.

Her colleagues noticed the change in her demeanor—she had become more withdrawn, more cautious. But Sarah couldn't afford to let anyone in on her secret. She had become a financial sleuth by necessity, and the weight of the truth she carried was a heavy burden.

As the weeks turned into months, the evidence they collected began to paint a chilling picture. Everest Corp's financial manipulation extended far beyond what Sarah had initially uncovered. It was a vast conspiracy involving high-ranking executives, external collaborators, and a network of offshore accounts designed to obscure the flow of illicit funds.

One evening, Sarah met David in a dimly lit parking garage. She handed him a USB drive containing the most damning evidence they had gathered so far. Her hands trembled as she did so, knowing that this small piece of technology held the power to expose Everest Corp's darkest secrets.

David examined the contents of the drive, his face etched with a mixture of satisfaction and concern. "This is it, Sarah. We have the smoking gun. But it's time to take our findings to the authorities. We can't continue this investigation on our own."

Sarah hesitated. She had known this moment would come, the moment when she would have to decide whether to go public with the evidence. But the fear of repercussions weighed heavily on her mind.

"What about protection?" she asked. "If we expose Everest Corp, they'll come after us with everything they have."

David nodded gravely. "I've already taken precautions. We have a contact within the SEC—a whistleblower protection program. They can offer us safety and legal immunity in exchange for the evidence."

Sarah took a deep breath, steeling herself for the decision she was about to make. "Let's do it. Let's expose them."

Their plan was set in motion. David made the necessary arrangements, ensuring that their identities would remain confidential. They handed over the USB drive to the SEC contact, who assured them that their evidence would be thoroughly investigated.

But as the days turned into weeks, Sarah couldn't shake the feeling of unease. The walls of secrecy that had protected her were closing in, and she knew that Everest Corp's powerful allies would stop at nothing to maintain their hold on the truth.

One evening, as Sarah was leaving her office, she received a call from an unknown number. She answered cautiously.

"Ms. Walker," a voice on the other end hissed, "you don't know what you've gotten yourself into. You should have stayed out of this."

Sarah's heart pounded in her chest as she realized the magnitude of the threat. Everest Corp had discovered her involvement in the investigation, and they were not about to let her expose their secrets without a fight.

The suspense that had simmered beneath the surface now boiled over into a dangerous game of cat and mouse. Sarah had crossed a line from which there was no turning back, and Everest Corp's web of deceit was closing in around her, threatening to ensnare her in a deadly trap of corporate power and deception.

Uncovering Clues

The city was drenched in the eerie glow of twilight, its streets shrouded in a thick mist that seemed to seep from the very pores of the skyscrapers. Sarah's footsteps echoed down the empty alley as she hurried toward the rendezvous point. Her breath formed ghostly clouds in the chilly air, and her heart pounded in her chest, a relentless reminder of the perilous path she had chosen.

David had called her earlier that day, his voice laced with urgency. "Meet me at the usual place, Sarah. We need to talk."

The usual place—a nondescript coffee shop tucked away in a quiet corner of the city—had been their sanctuary, their refuge from the prying eyes of Everest Corp. But tonight, Sarah sensed a shift in the winds of danger. She knew something had changed, something that could alter the course of their investigation.

As she pushed open the door to the cafe, the familiar scent of brewing coffee enveloped her. The few patrons scattered among the mismatched tables paid her no mind. Sarah had become adept at blending into the background, at disappearing into the tapestry of urban anonymity.

David was already seated at their usual table near the back, his eyes scanning the room with a cautious intensity. He looked up as Sarah approached, a silent acknowledgment passing between them.

"Sarah," he said in a hushed tone, "I've got news. Disturbing news."

She slid into the seat across from him, her heart pounding in anticipation. "What is it, David?"

He leaned in closer, his voice a whisper. "I received a tip—a reliable one. Everest Corp knows about our involvement with the SEC. They've launched an internal investigation to identify the whistleblower."

Sarah's blood ran cold. The threat she had feared had materialized. Everest Corp had caught wind of their activities, and now they were on the hunt. She couldn't help but feel a sense of dread, a realization that the shadowy figures behind the corporate giant would stop at nothing to protect their secrets.

"Are we compromised?" she asked, her voice trembling.

David nodded grimly. "It's possible. They have substantial resources, and if they connect the dots, they could trace it back to us. We need to be more careful than ever."

The weight of their situation settled on Sarah's shoulders like a leaden shroud. She had known the risks when she embarked on this journey, but the reality of facing a behemoth like Everest Corp was a daunting challenge that tested her resolve.

"What's our next move?" she asked, her voice filled with determination.

David's eyes bore into hers. "We need to accelerate our investigation. We can't rely solely on the SEC now. We have to gather as much evidence as we can, independently. If Everest Corp tries to shut us down, we'll have a backup plan."

Over the following weeks, Sarah and David redoubled their efforts to uncover the truth. They worked in secret, using encrypted communication channels and meeting in obscure locations. The tension in their lives escalated as they raced against time and the ever-present threat of discovery.

One evening, Sarah received an anonymous email with a cryptic message: "Follow the money, and you'll find the answers you seek." The message was accompanied by a series of seemingly innocuous financial transactions, each labeled with dates and amounts.

She couldn't shake the feeling that this was a breadcrumb trail, a clue left by an insider who wanted to expose Everest Corp's secrets. Sarah painstakingly traced the transactions, cross-referencing them with Everest Corp's financial records.

Late into the night, she made a breakthrough. The transactions led to a series of offshore accounts, hidden from prying eyes and auditors. These accounts were tied to a web of shell companies, each designed to obscure the flow of money.

The pieces of the puzzle began to fall into place. Everest Corp was not just inflating revenue; they were siphoning off millions of dollars into these hidden accounts. It was a carefully orchestrated scheme to enrich a select few at the expense of investors and employees.

Sarah's heart raced with excitement and trepidation. She had unearthed a crucial piece of evidence, one that could expose Everest Corp's financial malfeasance. But she also knew that time was running out. With Everest Corp's internal investigation closing in on them, they had to act quickly.

She met David in a dimly lit parking garage once again, her hands trembling as she handed over the evidence. "This is it, David. We have proof of the offshore accounts, the shell companies—everything."

David's eyes gleamed with a mixture of satisfaction and apprehension. "Good work, Sarah. We need to take this to the SEC immediately. It's our best chance at stopping Everest Corp."

But as they left the garage and made their way back to their respective lives, Sarah couldn't shake the feeling that they were playing a dangerous game, one with stakes higher than she had ever imagined. The knowledge she possessed was a double-edged sword, a weapon that could expose the truth but also put her life in peril.

The suspense of their investigation had reached a fever pitch, and the shadows of deceit loomed closer than ever. Everest Corp was on the hunt, and Sarah and David were caught in a deadly game of cat and mouse. The path they had chosen was fraught with danger, and there was no turning back now.

The Corporate Cover-Up

The relentless hum of fluorescent lights bathed Sarah's office in a cold, sterile glow. She sat at her desk, staring at the meticulously organized rows of financial documents on her computer screen. The evidence of Everest Corp's financial deception was laid out before her like a sinister jigsaw puzzle, each piece revealing a new layer of deceit.

It had been weeks since Sarah and David had handed over their evidence to the SEC, and the tension in her life had reached a boiling point. Every day felt like a countdown, a race against time before Everest Corp's internal investigation closed in on her. The walls of secrecy were closing in, and Sarah knew that her world was about to collide with the shadowy forces of corporate power.

A knock on her office door startled her. She quickly minimized the incriminating documents on her screen and composed herself before calling out, "Come in."

Her boss, Richard Stanton, stepped into the room, his suit impeccably tailored, his face a mask of practiced composure. Richard was a high-ranking executive at Everest Corp, and Sarah had always regarded him as a mentor and a friend. But now, with the weight of her secret bearing down on her, their interactions had taken on a new layer of complexity.

"Sarah," Richard said with a smile that didn't quite reach his eyes, "I wanted to check in on your progress with the audit. How's everything going?"

Sarah's heart raced as she met his gaze. She couldn't afford to betray any signs of her involvement in the investigation. "Everything's on track, Richard. I'm reviewing the financials as we speak. No major issues so far."

Richard nodded, but his eyes bore into hers, as if searching for any hint of deception. "Good to hear. Everest Corp takes its financial integrity very seriously, as you know."

The irony of his words hung in the air like a dark cloud. Everest Corp's commitment to financial integrity was precisely what Sarah had come to question, and she had the evidence to prove it. But she couldn't reveal her hand, not until the SEC had completed its investigation.

As Richard continued to ask probing questions about her audit, Sarah felt a growing sense of unease. It was as if he were testing her, probing for weaknesses in her facade. She knew she had to tread carefully, to maintain the appearance of business as usual, even as the walls of deceit closed in around her.

Days turned into weeks, and the suspense in Sarah's life became a suffocating presence. She continued to work diligently on her audit, all the while juggling secret meetings with David and a constant sense of paranoia. She couldn't escape the feeling that she was being watched, that every move she made was being scrutinized.

One evening, as Sarah left her office building, she noticed a black sedan parked across the street. It was a car she had seen before, one that seemed to appear wherever she went. She quickened her pace, her heart pounding in her chest, as she made her way to the subway station.

As she descended the stairs into the dimly lit station, she couldn't shake the feeling that she was being followed. She glanced over her shoulder, her breath catching in her throat as she saw a figure in a dark coat, shadowing her every step.

Panicking, Sarah quickened her pace, weaving through the crowded platform. She needed to lose her pursuer, to disappear into the labyrinth of tunnels beneath the city. But no matter how fast she moved, the figure remained close behind, a relentless presence in the shadows.

Sarah's mind raced, her heart pounding in her chest. She had to find a way out of this situation, to escape the clutches of whoever was following her. She spotted an approaching train and made a split-second decision. With a burst of adrenaline-fueled energy, she dashed through the closing doors just as the train pulled away from the platform.

Inside the crowded subway car, Sarah's breaths came in ragged gasps as she tried to compose herself. She had escaped her pursuer, at least for now. But the incident had shaken her to the core. Everest Corp was closing in, and the threat to her safety was real.

The next day, Sarah received an email from David, urging her to meet him urgently. She agreed to the meeting, knowing that they needed to assess the escalating danger they were facing.

They met in a dimly lit park, far from prying eyes and surveillance cameras. David's face was grave as he spoke, his words laced with concern. "Sarah, we can't afford to wait for the SEC any longer. Everest Corp knows we're onto them, and they're coming after us. We need to act now."

Sarah nodded, her determination clear. "What do you suggest?"

David handed her a small device, a burner phone. "Use this to contact our SEC contact directly. Tell them we have more evidence, and we need protection immediately. We can't trust Everest Corp to play fair."

As Sarah took the burner phone, a sense of urgency surged through her. She knew that their investigation had reached a critical juncture, and their lives were hanging in the balance. She dialed the number for their SEC contact and arranged a meeting to deliver the additional evidence.

But as she left the park that evening, a feeling of unease settled over her. The shadows of suspense and danger were closing in, and the corporate giant they had dared to challenge was poised to strike back with all the resources at its disposal.

Sarah's life had become a high-stakes game, one where every move carried the risk of exposure and betrayal. The investigation she had embarked upon had taken a perilous turn, and the consequences of her pursuit of truth were becoming all too real. There was no turning back now, not when the corporate cover-up had transformed into a deadly cat-and-mouse chase.

Partners in Crime

The night air was thick with tension as Sarah made her way to the designated meeting spot. A narrow alleyway, shrouded in darkness, seemed like the perfect place for a clandestine exchange. Her heart raced, and every rustling leaf and passing shadow heightened her sense of paranoia. She clutched the burner phone tightly in her hand, her lifeline to the SEC contact who could provide protection.

David had warned her to trust no one, and she had taken his words to heart. The mole within Everest Corp who had sent her the anonymous email had provided crucial information, but she couldn't be certain of their true intentions. Betrayal was a constant specter looming over her.

As Sarah reached the alleyway, she saw a figure waiting in the shadows. The dim glow of a streetlight revealed the silhouette of a man, his face obscured by a hood. Her pulse quickened, and she approached cautiously, her senses on high alert.

The man stepped forward, his voice a low whisper. "You're Sarah?"

She nodded, her voice barely above a murmur. "Yes. You're the one who contacted me?"

He nodded. "I've been keeping tabs on Everest Corp for a while. What you've uncovered—the offshore accounts, the shell companies—it's just the tip of the iceberg. There's more, much more."

Sarah felt a glimmer of hope. If this insider had additional information, it could be the key to unraveling the corporate conspiracy once and for all. But she couldn't afford to let her guard down.

"What else do you know?" she asked, her voice steady.

The insider hesitated before continuing. "There's a group within Everest Corp—a tight-knit circle of executives and external partners. They call themselves 'The Syndicate.' They control everything—the fraudulent transactions, the cover-ups. They're the puppet masters behind it all."

Sarah's heart sank at the mention of The Syndicate. It was a term she had come across in her research, a shadowy cabal rumored to pull the strings behind Everest Corp's financial manipulation. If what the insider was saying was true, then The Syndicate was the linchpin holding the entire conspiracy together.

"I need proof," Sarah said, her voice determined. "Concrete evidence that ties The Syndicate to the fraud."

The insider nodded. "I can get you what you need, but it won't be easy. They're careful, cautious. They've silenced anyone who's crossed them before."

Sarah's mind raced, contemplating the risks. She had already ventured into dangerous territory, but exposing The Syndicate would be the final blow to Everest Corp's deceptive empire. She needed that evidence, no matter the cost.

"Get me the proof," she said firmly, "and I'll make sure it reaches the right hands."

The insider handed her a small envelope containing a flash drive. "This is just the beginning. There are more secrets buried deep within Everest Corp. Be careful, Sarah. They'll stop at nothing to protect The Syndicate."

With that, the insider disappeared into the shadows, leaving Sarah alone in the alleyway. She clutched the envelope tightly, a mixture of determination and fear coursing through her veins. The suspense of their investigation had taken a perilous turn, plunging her deeper into the labyrinth of corporate deception.

Over the next few days, Sarah analyzed the contents of the flash drive in secret. The evidence it contained was damning—emails, financial records, and encrypted communications that pointed to the existence of The Syndicate within Everest Corp. She knew that this information could expose the heart of the conspiracy.

But as she delved deeper into the web of deceit, she became acutely aware of the danger she was in. Everest Corp's internal investigation was closing in on her, and she could feel the weight of their scrutiny bearing down. She had to be meticulous, to leave no trace of her activities, and to protect the identity of the insider who had risked everything to provide the evidence.

One evening, as Sarah was leaving her office, she received a text message from David: "Meet me tonight. Urgent."

She replied with a single word: "Where?"

David's response came quickly: "The abandoned warehouse on 12th Street. Midnight."

Sarah knew that this meeting was different, that something had changed. The urgency in David's message was palpable, and she couldn't shake the feeling that their investigation was reaching its climax.

As the clock struck midnight, Sarah arrived at the desolate warehouse. Its windows were shattered, and the moonlight cast eerie shadows on the broken concrete floor. The air was thick with anticipation as she scanned the darkness for any sign of David.

He emerged from the shadows, his face etched with a mixture of exhaustion and determination. "Sarah," he said, his voice barely a whisper, "we've run out of time. Everest Corp's internal investigation is closing in on us. We need to expose The Syndicate now, before they can silence us."

She nodded, her resolve unwavering. "I have the evidence, David. It's on a secure server, encrypted and backed up in multiple locations. If anything happens to us, the information will be released to the world."

David's eyes gleamed with a fierce determination. "Good. Let's make our move."

Together, they devised a plan to expose The Syndicate. They would arrange a meeting with the SEC contact, provide the evidence, and go public with their findings. The time for secrecy was over, and the suspense of their investigation had reached its zenith.

But as they left the abandoned warehouse and made their way through the darkened streets, a sense of foreboding settled over Sarah. The corporate cover-up was unraveling, and The Syndicate's grip on Everest Corp was weakening. But the danger they faced had never been greater, and the shadows of suspense and deception loomed closer than ever.

Sarah's life had become a high-stakes gamble, one where the odds were stacked against her. The pursuit of truth had brought her to the precipice of danger, and the consequences of her actions were about to be realized. There was no turning back now, not when the fate of Everest Corp's hidden empire hung in the balance.

A Trail of Destruction

The city was cloaked in darkness as Sarah and David huddled in the dimly lit corner of a nondescript cafe. The scent of brewing coffee masked their hushed conversation as they planned their next move. The evidence they possessed, the key to exposing The Syndicate within Everest Corp, weighed heavily on their minds.

"We can't delay any longer," David said, his voice low but resolute. "We need to set up a meeting with the SEC contact and deliver the evidence."

Sarah nodded, her eyes reflecting a mix of determination and anxiety. "I've already made arrangements. The meeting is set for tomorrow night, in a secure location. We'll hand over everything we have."

The stakes had never been higher. Everest Corp was closing in, their internal investigation fueled by a growing sense of desperation. The Syndicate, the shadowy cabal behind the corporate conspiracy, had powerful allies, and they would stop at nothing to protect their interests.

As Sarah and David left the cafe, the suspense of their investigation hung in the air like a storm on the horizon. They knew that their lives were in danger, that the path they had chosen was fraught with peril. But there was no turning back now, not when the truth was within their grasp.

The following night, they met with their SEC contact in a secure, undisclosed location. The contact, a seasoned investigator with a steely resolve, reviewed the evidence meticulously, his face growing grimmer with each revelation.

"This is damning," he said, his voice a low murmur. "If we can verify the authenticity of these documents, Everest Corp will face one of the most significant corporate scandals in history."

Sarah and David exchanged glances, a mixture of relief and trepidation washing over them. The evidence they had gathered over months of clandestine investigations had the power to shatter Everest Corp's facade of financial integrity.

The SEC contact continued, "We'll need to move quickly. I'll initiate an internal investigation within the SEC to maintain the secrecy of our sources. We can't afford any leaks."

Sarah nodded, her determination unwavering. "Just ensure that the evidence is protected. Everest Corp will do everything in their power to discredit us and destroy the proof."

Their meeting concluded, and Sarah and David left the secure location, their hearts heavy with the knowledge that the corporate giant they had challenged was about to be exposed. The suspense of their investigation had reached its zenith, and the consequences of their actions were about to unfold.

But as they made their way through the city streets, a sense of foreboding settled over Sarah. She couldn't shake the feeling that they were being watched, that Everest Corp's powerful allies were closing in, ready to strike back with all the resources at their disposal.

The days that followed were a whirlwind of anxiety and anticipation. The SEC contact assured them that the investigation was progressing, but the wheels of bureaucracy moved slowly, and the suspense of waiting weighed heavily on Sarah and David.

Then, one evening, as Sarah returned to her apartment after a meeting with David, she noticed something amiss. The door to her apartment was slightly ajar, a faint beam of light spilling into the hallway. Panic gripped her as she cautiously pushed open the door and entered her home.

Her heart pounded in her chest as she realized that her apartment had been ransacked. Drawers lay open, papers were scattered across the floor, and her computer had been tampered with. It was a clear message, a warning that her pursuit of truth had not gone unnoticed.

With trembling hands, Sarah quickly gathered what evidence she could, stashing it in a hidden compartment in her closet. She knew that Everest Corp's agents had breached her sanctuary, that her life was in grave danger.

As she left her apartment, the feeling of vulnerability gnawed at her. She couldn't return there, not when her home had become a crime scene. She needed to find a safe place to regroup, to continue their fight against The Syndicate.

Sarah met David in a dimly lit park, their faces reflecting the weight of the situation. "My apartment was compromised," she said, her voice strained. "They know we're onto them."

David clenched his fists, his anger simmering beneath the surface. "We can't stay here. We need to disappear, go off the grid. Everest Corp's reach is vast, and they won't stop until they've silenced us."

Sarah nodded in agreement. "We'll need to rely on our contacts, the ones who have helped us so far. They can provide us with a safe place to regroup."

Their decision made, Sarah and David set in motion a plan to disappear, to go underground and protect the evidence they had gathered. The suspense of their investigation had escalated into a high-stakes game of survival, and the shadowy forces of corporate power were closing in with relentless determination.

The next few days were a blur of clandestine meetings, encrypted communications, and constant vigilance. Sarah and David relied on a network of trusted allies to stay hidden, moving from one safe location to another, always one step ahead of their pursuers.

But as they eluded capture, the suspense of their investigation reached a fever pitch. The evidence they possessed, the key to exposing The Syndicate, became a coveted prize in a dangerous game of cat and mouse.

The shadows of deception and danger loomed closer than ever, and Sarah and David knew that the final showdown with Everest Corp and The Syndicate was inevitable. The suspense of their investigation had transformed into a life-and-death struggle, and there was no turning back now, not when the truth was within their grasp.

The Hunter Becomes the Hunted

The moon hung low in the night sky, casting long shadows over the abandoned warehouse where Sarah and David had taken refuge. The damp air clung to their skin as they huddled in the darkness, their breaths shallow with anxiety. The suspense of their investigation had escalated into a relentless pursuit, and Everest Corp's relentless agents were closing in.

David's face was etched with worry as he spoke in hushed tones. "They're getting closer, Sarah. We can't stay here much longer. We need a plan, a way to expose The Syndicate without putting ourselves in even greater danger."

Sarah nodded, her thoughts racing. The evidence they had gathered was a ticking time bomb, a weapon that could bring down Everest Corp's empire of deceit. But they needed a way to detonate it safely, to ensure that their lives weren't collateral damage in the explosion.

"I've been thinking," she said, her voice low and determined, "what if we use a trusted journalist to leak the evidence? Someone who can't be easily silenced, someone with a reputation for exposing corporate corruption."

David considered her suggestion. "It's risky, but it could work. We'll need to find the right journalist, someone who can protect their sources and has the resources to investigate further."

Their plan set in motion, they reached out to their network of contacts, searching for a journalist who could help them expose The Syndicate. It was a perilous endeavor, and they knew that the consequences of their actions could be deadly.

Days turned into weeks as they continued to elude capture, moving from one safe location to another. The suspense of their investigation was a constant presence, a shadowy specter that haunted their every move. Everest Corp's relentless pursuit showed no sign of relenting, and The Syndicate's reach seemed boundless.

Then, one evening, they received a message from a contact they had almost forgotten—a journalist named Elena Chavez. Her reputation for fearless investigative reporting and her commitment to exposing corporate corruption made her the perfect ally.

They arranged a meeting with Elena in a secluded park, their faces hidden in the shadows as they discussed their plan. She listened intently as they explained the evidence they possessed and the danger they faced.

"I've exposed powerful corporations before," Elena said, her voice unwavering. "I have contacts in the media who can help me get the story out. But we need to be careful, meticulous. The Syndicate won't hesitate to come after us."

Sarah and David nodded in agreement. They knew that their lives were on the line, that Everest Corp's agents and The Syndicate's enforcers were closing in with relentless determination.

Over the next few days, they worked closely with Elena, providing her with the evidence and guiding her through the web of deceit that had ensnared Everest Corp. The suspense of their investigation had reached its climax, and they could feel the weight of the truth about to be exposed.

Then, one fateful night, as they prepared to hand over the final pieces of evidence to Elena, disaster struck. A sudden, blinding flash of light illuminated the abandoned warehouse, followed by the deafening roar of an explosion. The shockwave sent them sprawling to the ground, their ears ringing, and the acrid smell of smoke filling the air.

As they struggled to their feet, they saw the warehouse engulfed in flames, the evidence they had gathered now reduced to ashes. Their plans had been sabotaged, their lifeline to the truth incinerated in an instant.

Sarah's heart sank as she realized the gravity of the situation. Everest Corp had found them, had launched a devastating attack to eliminate the evidence and anyone who possessed it. The suspense of their investigation had spiraled into a deadly showdown, and they were the ones in the crosshairs.

With smoke billowing around them, they fled the burning warehouse, their minds racing to find an escape route. They knew that they were no match for Everest Corp's firepower, that their lives were hanging by a thread.

As they emerged into the night, they saw a black SUV waiting in the distance, its engine idling. The vehicle was unmarked, a silent harbinger of their impending doom.

"We have to split up," David said urgently. "I'll create a diversion, draw them away from you. Head for the safehouse we discussed with Elena. It's your best chance."

Sarah nodded, her heart heavy with the knowledge that they were about to be separated. She watched as David sprinted in the opposite direction, disappearing into the darkness, a lone figure determined to buy her time.

She raced toward the waiting SUV, her heart pounding in her chest, her every step echoing with the suspense of their desperate flight. As she climbed into the vehicle, the driver hit the gas pedal, and they sped away from the burning warehouse, leaving behind the ruins of their investigation.

The pursuit was relentless, the danger omnipresent. Sarah knew that the hunter had become the hunted, that Everest Corp's agents were closing in with ruthless determination. The suspense of their investigation had transformed into a high-stakes battle for survival, and there was no turning back now, not when the truth remained just out of reach.

The Deadly Chase

The black SUV raced through the labyrinthine streets of the city, weaving through traffic with reckless abandon. Sarah's heart hammered in her chest as she clung to the seat, her mind racing with a single thought: escape. The suspense of their deadly pursuit hung over her like a storm, and Everest Corp's relentless agents were closing in with ruthless determination.

The driver, a silent and stoic figure, navigated the urban maze with the precision of a seasoned professional. Sarah had no doubt that they were part of the network Elena had arranged to help her disappear, but she couldn't shake the feeling that their pursuers were hot on their trail.

As the SUV sped through a narrow alley, Sarah caught a glimpse of a black sedan in the rearview mirror, its windows tinted, its occupants hidden from view. It was the same vehicle that had followed her before, a relentless shadow in her life.

"They're still following us," she said, her voice tense.

The driver's eyes flicked to the rearview mirror, and Sarah saw a flash of concern in their expression. "We need to lose them."

The chase intensified as the SUV darted through a series of winding streets, each turn designed to shake off their pursuers. But the black sedan remained doggedly persistent, closing the gap with every maneuver.

Sarah's pulse quickened as she realized the gravity of the situation. Everest Corp's agents were not giving up, and they would stop at nothing to eliminate her and the evidence she possessed. The suspense of their deadly pursuit had reached its peak, and her life hung in the balance.

Then, as they approached a crowded market square, chaos erupted. A cacophony of horns, shouts, and the blaring sirens of police cars filled the air. The black sedan swerved to avoid a collision, its driver losing precious seconds in the process.

The driver of the SUV seized the opportunity, accelerating through the narrow streets of the market, narrowly avoiding pedestrians and stalls. Sarah's heart raced as they weaved through the labyrinth of obstacles, the suspense of their escape a white-knuckle ride.

But as they emerged from the market, Sarah's sense of relief was short-lived. The black sedan had not given up the chase, and it was gaining ground once more. The relentless pursuit showed no sign of relenting, and she knew that her life was still in grave danger.

"We need a plan," she said, her voice determined. "We can't outrun them forever."

The driver nodded, their eyes scanning the streets ahead. "There's a safehouse nearby. We can lose them there and regroup."

With a sense of urgency, the SUV veered off the main road and into a network of narrow alleyways. Sarah watched as the black sedan followed suit, its occupants relentless in their pursuit.

But as they approached the safehouse, the driver executed a sudden, unexpected maneuver. They swerved into a dead-end alley, their tires screeching as they came to a stop. The black sedan, caught off guard, skidded to a halt just behind them.

Before Sarah could react, the driver leaped out of the SUV, a determined look in their eyes. "Get out and follow me. We have to move quickly."

Sarah complied, her heart pounding, as she followed the driver into a maze of interconnected buildings and hidden passageways. The suspense of their escape had taken an unexpected turn, and she could feel the adrenaline surging through her veins.

They moved swiftly through the labyrinthine alleys, the sound of their pursuers growing distant. The driver led her to a nondescript door, which opened into a dimly lit safehouse.

Inside, Sarah found Elena waiting, her expression a mix of relief and concern. "I heard what happened. Are you alright?"

Sarah nodded, her breath still ragged from the chase. "We need to act quickly. The evidence is gone, but we can still expose The Syndicate. We just need a plan."

Elena's eyes gleamed with determination. "We have contacts in the media who can help us get the word out. But we'll need solid leads, corroborating evidence, something that can't be discredited."

Sarah knew that their window of opportunity was closing fast. Everest Corp's agents were relentless, and they would regroup and come after her with even greater determination.

"We have to find someone on the inside," she said, her voice resolute.

"Someone who can testify, someone who knows the inner workings of The Syndicate."

Elena nodded in agreement. "I'll reach out to my contacts. We'll dig deeper, expose every connection, and bring The Syndicate to light."

As they began to formulate their plan, Sarah couldn't escape the feeling that they were racing against time, that the suspense of their investigation had reached a critical juncture. The danger they faced was undeniable, but the pursuit of truth had become a relentless force, a determination to expose the shadowy cabal behind Everest Corp's corporate conspiracy.

The days that followed were a whirlwind of covert meetings, encrypted communications, and painstaking investigations. Sarah and Elena worked tirelessly to uncover the identities of those within Everest Corp who could testify against The Syndicate. The suspense of their pursuit was unrelenting, but they knew that they were closing in on the truth.

Then, one evening, as they sifted through a trove of encrypted documents, they found a breakthrough—a series of emails that hinted at a high-ranking executive within Everest Corp who had grown disillusioned with The Syndicate's machinations. It was a lead, a potential witness who could expose the inner workings of the shadowy cabal.

With their new evidence in hand, Sarah and Elena reached out to the contact, arranging a meeting in a secure, undisclosed location. The suspense of their investigation had reached a fever pitch, and they could feel the weight of The Syndicate's secrets about to be exposed.

As they prepared for the meeting, Sarah couldn't escape the feeling that their pursuit had brought them to the brink of a precipice, that the final confrontation with Everest Corp and The Syndicate was imminent. The suspense of their investigation had transformed into a relentless quest for justice, and there was no turning back now, not when the truth was within their grasp.

The Testimony

The night was shrouded in darkness as Sarah and Elena made their way to the predetermined meeting location, a discreet underground parking garage that provided a modicum of cover from prying eyes. The suspense of the impending meeting weighed heavily on them, their steps echoing in the empty concrete space.

Elena's voice was hushed as she spoke, her breath visible in the chilly air. "Are you sure this contact can be trusted, Sarah? We're placing everything on this testimony."

Sarah nodded, her determination unwavering. "I've vetted them thoroughly. They've been disillusioned with The Syndicate for a long time, and they want to see justice served. This is our chance to expose the truth."

Their contact, a high-ranking executive within Everest Corp, had agreed to provide testimony that could unravel The Syndicate's grip on the corporate giant. It was a perilous endeavor, one that carried grave risks, but the pursuit of truth had become an unrelenting force, a determination to bring the shadowy cabal to justice.

As they reached the designated spot within the parking garage, Sarah couldn't shake the feeling of vulnerability. Everest Corp's agents were relentless, and they would stop at nothing to protect The Syndicate's secrets. The suspense of the impending meeting hung over her like a storm.

Moments later, a figure emerged from the shadows, their face obscured by a hood. The contact's voice was tense as they spoke, their words measured and deliberate. "You have the evidence?"

Sarah nodded, producing a secure device containing the corroborating documents they had uncovered. "This is everything we've gathered. It's the key to exposing The Syndicate's inner workings."

The contact accepted the device, their gloved hands trembling with a mix of fear and determination. "I'll testify, but you need to protect me. They have eyes and ears everywhere, and they won't hesitate to silence me."

Elena stepped forward, her voice resolute. "We have a network of allies, lawyers, and journalists who will ensure your safety. But we need to move quickly, before Everest Corp can react."

The contact nodded, a sense of urgency in their eyes. "I'll provide the testimony, but you need to make sure it reaches the right authorities."

Their agreement reached, they parted ways, each burdened with the gravity of their roles in the impending expose. The suspense of their investigation had transformed into a race against time, a battle against the forces of corporate power.

Over the next few days, Sarah and Elena worked tirelessly to prepare for the testimony. They reached out to their network of allies, coordinating with lawyers and journalists who were committed to bringing The Syndicate to light. The suspense of their impending expose was palpable, and they knew that Everest Corp would stop at nothing to protect their secrets.

Then, the day of the testimony arrived—a high-stakes showdown between the pursuit of truth and the shadowy forces of corporate power. The location was a secure, undisclosed courtroom, with witnesses placed under protection to shield them from retaliation.

Sarah watched as the contact took the stand, their voice steady, their resolve unwavering. They began to testify about The Syndicate, revealing the inner workings of the shadowy cabal that had manipulated Everest Corp's financial empire. The suspense in the courtroom was palpable, a tension that hung in the air like a heavy fog.

As the testimony unfolded, Sarah couldn't help but feel a sense of vindication. The evidence they had gathered, the corroborating documents, and the testimony of their contact were painting a damning portrait of Everest Corp's corruption. The suspense of the expose was reaching its climax, and the consequences of their actions were about to unfold.

But as the testimony continued, a sense of unease settled over Sarah. She couldn't shake the feeling that Everest Corp's agents were present in the courtroom, that their network of spies and enforcers was poised to strike back.

Then, as the contact reached a pivotal moment in their testimony, chaos erupted. The courtroom doors burst open, and armed security personnel stormed in, their weapons drawn. They moved with ruthless precision, taking control of the situation with brutal force.

Sarah's heart pounded as she realized the gravity of the situation. Everest Corp had infiltrated the courtroom, and they were determined to silence the testimony, to protect The Syndicate's secrets at all costs. The suspense of the expose had taken a deadly turn, and their lives were now hanging by a thread.

Elena grabbed Sarah's arm, her voice urgent. "We need to get out of here. Now!"

With a sense of desperation, they made their way to a side exit, slipping through a maze of corridors and stairwells. The suspense of their escape was a relentless force, a determination to elude Everest Corp's agents and protect the testimony that could expose The Syndicate.

As they emerged into the cool night air, Sarah's mind raced. They had narrowly escaped capture, but the testimony had been compromised, and their contact was in grave danger. The suspense of their investigation had taken a perilous turn, and the battle against corporate corruption had become a fight for survival.

They regrouped with their network of allies, working tirelessly to ensure the safety of their contact and to protect the evidence they had gathered. The suspense of their expose was far from over, and the shadows of deception and danger loomed closer than ever.

In the days that followed, they continued to pursue the truth, determined to expose The Syndicate and bring Everest Corp to justice. The suspense of their investigation had become an unrelenting force, a testament to their unwavering commitment to exposing the darkest secrets of corporate power.

As Sarah and Elena pressed forward, they knew that the battle was far from over, that Everest Corp's agents and The Syndicate's enforcers were still determined to protect their empire of deceit. The suspense of their pursuit was unyielding, but they remained steadfast, knowing that the pursuit of truth was a fight worth every sacrifice.

The Final Gambit

The night hung heavy with tension as Sarah and Elena gathered with their network of allies in a clandestine safehouse. The recent courtroom debacle had been a sobering reminder of Everest Corp's unrelenting power and their determination to protect The Syndicate's secrets. The suspense of their investigation had become a perilous dance with danger, and the stakes had never been higher.

Elena's voice was resolute as she addressed the group. "We can't afford any more setbacks. We need to find another way to expose The Syndicate and bring Everest Corp to justice."

The room was filled with nods of agreement, the determination to see their mission through unwavering. The evidence they had gathered, the testimony they had hoped to use, had been compromised, but they knew that the truth could not remain hidden forever.

Sarah spoke up, her voice steady. "We need a new strategy, a way to expose The Syndicate that Everest Corp can't thwart. We have to be one step ahead of them."

As they discussed their options, a plan began to take shape—an audacious gambit that would force The Syndicate's hand and expose their secrets to the world. It was a high-stakes endeavor, one that carried immense risks, but the suspense of their investigation had brought them to a point of no return.

The plan involved a two-pronged approach. First, they would enlist the help of a renowned investigative journalist known for their fearless exposés. The journalist would write an incisive article that would cast a spotlight on Everest Corp and The Syndicate, using the evidence they had gathered to substantiate their claims.

Second, they would orchestrate a coordinated social media campaign, one that would go viral and draw global attention to the article. The goal was to ensure that the truth could not be silenced, that The Syndicate's secrets would be exposed on a massive scale.

Over the following weeks, they set their plan in motion. Sarah and Elena worked closely with the journalist, providing them with the evidence and helping them craft a narrative that would captivate the public's imagination. The suspense of their operation was palpable, as they knew that Everest Corp's agents would stop at nothing to prevent the truth from coming to light.

As the article neared completion, the suspense among their allies grew. They had assembled a dedicated team of activists, hackers, and social media experts to ensure the campaign's success. The battle against corporate corruption had become a global cause, and they were determined to see it through to the end.

Then, the day of the article's release arrived—a day that would either mark the downfall of Everest Corp and The Syndicate or the final, devastating blow against Sarah and her allies. The suspense in the safehouse was electric as they watched the journalist's byline appear on news websites around the world.

The article was a masterstroke of investigative journalism, a searing indictment of Everest Corp's corruption and The Syndicate's machinations. It exposed the inner workings of the shadowy cabal, using the evidence they had gathered to paint a damning picture of corporate greed and deception.

As the article spread like wildfire across social media, the suspense of their campaign reached its zenith. #ExposeTheSyndicate trended worldwide, drawing attention from activists, journalists, and concerned citizens. Everest Corp's agents scrambled to contain the fallout, but the truth was out, and it couldn't be silenced.

The days that followed were a whirlwind of media attention, as news outlets around the world picked up the story. Corporate whistleblowers came forward, confirming the allegations against Everest Corp and The Syndicate. The suspense of their investigation had transformed into a global reckoning, a moment of truth that could not be denied.

But Everest Corp was not defeated yet. They launched a counteroffensive, employing an army of lawyers, lobbyists, and public relations experts to discredit the allegations and salvage their reputation. The suspense of the battle raged on, a relentless struggle for the hearts and minds of the public.

As the weeks turned into months, Sarah and her allies remained vigilant, determined to see their mission through to the end. The suspense of the expose had revealed the darkest secrets of corporate power, and the world was watching.

Then, one evening, as Sarah was reviewing the latest developments in the campaign, she received a message from their contact within Everest Corp—the one who had risked everything to provide the initial evidence. The message was brief but urgent:

"They're coming after me. I need protection."

The suspense of the message sent a chill down Sarah's spine. Everest Corp's agents were closing in on their contact, and their life was in grave danger. Without their testimony, the case against The Syndicate would be significantly weakened.

Sarah knew that they had to act quickly. She reached out to their network of allies, coordinating a plan to extract their contact from Everest Corp's grasp. The suspense of the rescue mission was a relentless force, a determination to protect the key witness in their battle against corporate corruption.

As the operation unfolded, Sarah couldn't escape the feeling that Everest Corp's agents were always one step ahead, that the suspense of their investigation had brought them to the brink of a final, deadly showdown.

The rescue mission was a high-stakes endeavor, fraught with danger and uncertainty. They encountered obstacles and adversaries at every turn, but their determination to protect their contact never wavered.

Finally, they succeeded in extracting their contact from Everest Corp's clutches, whisking them away to a secure location. The suspense of the mission had taken a toll, but their key witness was safe, and their battle against The Syndicate could continue.

As they regrouped, Sarah couldn't help but feel that the suspense of their investigation had brought them to a pivotal moment. Everest Corp was wounded, but not defeated, and The Syndicate still had powerful allies. The battle against corporate corruption was far from over, and the final gambit had yet to be played.

The suspense of their pursuit remained unyielding, a testament to their unwavering commitment to the pursuit of truth. The shadows of deception and danger still loomed closer than ever, and Sarah knew that the ultimate showdown was inevitable.

But they would not back down, not when the truth was within their grasp. The suspense of their investigation had become a relentless force, a determination to see justice served, no matter the cost.

The Showdown

The suspense hung thick in the air as Sarah and her allies gathered in a secure location, their faces etched with determination. They had weathered the storm of their campaign, exposing The Syndicate's secrets to the world and dealing a blow to Everest Corp's empire of deceit. But the battle against corporate corruption was far from over, and the final showdown loomed like a thundercloud on the horizon.

Their contact, the key witness who had risked everything to provide evidence against The Syndicate, sat nervously in the dimly lit room. The recent attempt on their life had left them shaken, but their resolve remained unyielding.

Elena spoke up, her voice resolute. "We have to ensure their safety and make sure their testimony is protected. Everest Corp will stop at nothing to silence them."

The room was filled with nods of agreement, the determination to see their mission through unwavering. The suspense of the impending showdown weighed heavily on them, but they knew that the pursuit of truth was a battle worth fighting.

Their plan was simple yet audacious: they would arrange for their contact to testify before a congressional committee, ensuring that their testimony would be protected by legal safeguards. It was a dangerous gambit, one that would expose The Syndicate's secrets in a public forum, but it was their best chance to bring Everest Corp to justice.

Over the following days, they worked tirelessly to coordinate the logistics of the testimony, reaching out to sympathetic members of Congress who were committed to exposing corporate corruption. The suspense of their operation was palpable, as they knew that Everest Corp's agents would stop at nothing to prevent the truth from being revealed.

The day of the congressional hearing arrived—a day that would either mark the downfall of Everest Corp and The Syndicate or the final, devastating blow against Sarah and her allies. The suspense in the committee room was electric as they watched their contact take the oath, their voice steady, their resolve unwavering.

As the testimony began, the room was filled with lawmakers, journalists, and concerned citizens, all eager to hear the key witness expose The Syndicate's secrets. The suspense of the hearing was palpable, as the testimony painted a damning picture of corporate greed and deception.

But Everest Corp was not defeated yet. They had assembled a team of high-powered lawyers, lobbyists, and public relations experts to discredit the allegations and salvage their reputation. The suspense of the battle raged on, a relentless struggle for the hearts and minds of the public.

As the testimony continued, a sense of unease settled over Sarah. She couldn't shake the feeling that Everest Corp's agents were present in the room, that their network of spies and enforcers was poised to strike back.

Then, as the key witness reached a pivotal moment in their testimony, chaos erupted. A commotion at the back of the room drew everyone's attention, and Sarah's heart sank as she saw a group of armed security personnel storming in, their weapons drawn.

The suspense in the committee room escalated into a full-blown confrontation as the security personnel attempted to halt the testimony. Lawmakers and activists rushed to protect the key witness, their determination to see the truth exposed unwavering.

Sarah watched as the standoff unfolded, a tense standoff between those who sought justice and those who sought to protect The Syndicate's secrets. The suspense of the showdown was a relentless force, a determination to see their mission through to the end.

Then, the unexpected happened—a high-ranking member of Congress, sympathetic to their cause, took the floor and demanded that the testimony continue. The room fell silent as they passionately defended the importance of exposing corporate corruption and protecting whistleblowers.

The suspense in the room reached its zenith as the lawmaker's words resonated with the audience, swaying public opinion in their favor. Everest Corp's attempt to thwart the testimony had backfired, and the truth could not be silenced.

The key witness continued their testimony, their voice unwavering, their resolve unbreakable. The suspense of the hearing had reached a critical juncture, and the consequences of their actions were about to unfold.

As the hearing concluded, Sarah couldn't escape the feeling that they had won a battle but not the war. Everest Corp was wounded, but not defeated, and The Syndicate still had powerful allies. The suspense of their investigation had brought them to a pivotal moment, and the ultimate showdown was imminent.

The days that followed were a whirlwind of media attention, as news outlets around the world covered the explosive congressional hearing. Corporate whistleblowers came forward, confirming the allegations against Everest Corp and The Syndicate. The suspense of their investigation had transformed into a global reckoning, a moment of truth that could not be denied.

But Everest Corp was not giving up. They launched a final counteroffensive, using all their resources to discredit the allegations and protect their interests. The suspense of the battle raged on, a relentless struggle for the future of corporate accountability.

Sarah and her allies remained vigilant, determined to see their mission through to the end. The suspense of the investigation had become a relentless force, a testament to their unwavering commitment to the pursuit of truth. The shadows of deception and danger still loomed closer than ever, and the ultimate showdown was inevitable.

As they pressed forward, they knew that Everest Corp's agents and The Syndicate's enforcers were still determined to protect their empire of deceit. The suspense of their pursuit remained unyielding, but they remained steadfast, knowing that the pursuit of truth was a fight worth every sacrifice.

The final chapter of their investigation had yet to be written, and the suspense of their battle against corporate corruption would carry them to the brink of a new beginning.

Unveiling the Conspiracy

The suspense that had gripped Sarah and her allies for months was now reaching its crescendo. The battle against corporate corruption had evolved into a relentless struggle to expose The Syndicate and bring Everest Corp to justice. As they faced the final chapter of their investigation, they knew that the ultimate showdown was imminent.

Sarah, Elena, and their contact, the key witness who had risked everything to expose The Syndicate's secrets, sat in a secure location, surrounded by a team of lawyers and activists. They had weathered countless obstacles, confronted danger head-on, and now faced their greatest challenge—the legal battle that would determine the fate of Everest Corp and The Syndicate.

The courtroom was a hushed and solemn place, its atmosphere charged with anticipation. The suspense in the air was palpable, as they watched the legal teams prepare for the trial that would decide the destiny of corporate accountability.

The prosecution, led by a tenacious and principled attorney, was ready to present their case against Everest Corp and The Syndicate. The defense, a formidable team of high-powered lawyers hired by Everest Corp, was equally prepared to protect their interests and discredit the allegations.

The judge entered the courtroom, signaling the start of the trial. Sarah watched as the key witness took the stand, their face obscured by shadows to protect their identity. The suspense of the moment was a heavy weight on their shoulders, as they prepared to expose The Syndicate's secrets on the grandest stage.

The prosecution's opening statement was a powerful indictment of Everest Corp's corruption, using the evidence they had gathered to paint a damning picture of corporate greed and deception. The suspense in the courtroom was electric, as journalists, lawmakers, and concerned citizens filled the seats, eager to witness the trial of the century.

But Everest Corp's defense team was not to be underestimated. They launched a counteroffensive, employing every legal maneuver and tactic to discredit the allegations and protect their interests. The suspense of the legal battle was a relentless struggle for the truth, as both sides fought to control the narrative.

As the trial unfolded, Sarah couldn't escape the feeling that Everest Corp's agents were still present, lurking in the shadows, ready to strike back. The suspense of their investigation had transformed into a high-stakes legal showdown, and the consequences of their actions were about to unfold.

The key witness's testimony was a pivotal moment in the trial, as they revealed the inner workings of The Syndicate and the extent of Everest Corp's involvement. The suspense in the courtroom was palpable, as their words resonated with the audience, swaying public opinion in favor of corporate accountability.

But Everest Corp's defense team launched a fierce cross-examination, attempting to undermine the witness's credibility and cast doubt on their claims. The suspense of the legal battle raged on, a relentless struggle for the future of corporate accountability.

As the trial continued, Sarah and her allies remained vigilant, determined to see their mission through to the end. The suspense of the investigation had become a relentless force, a testament to their unwavering commitment to the pursuit of truth.

Then, an unexpected turn of events shifted the balance of the trial. A surprise witness emerged, a former high-ranking executive within Everest Corp who had grown disillusioned with The Syndicate's machinations. Their testimony corroborated the key witness's claims and provided damning evidence against the corporation.

The suspense in the courtroom reached its zenith as the surprise witness took the stand, their voice unwavering, their resolve unbreakable. The truth could no longer be denied, and the fate of Everest Corp and The Syndicate hung in the balance.

As the trial reached its climax, Sarah watched as Everest Corp's defense team launched a final, desperate attempt to salvage their reputation. But the evidence against them was overwhelming, and the suspense of the legal battle had become a relentless force for corporate accountability.

Then, the jury began their deliberations, the suspense in the courtroom unbearable as they weighed the evidence and considered their verdict. Sarah, Elena, and their allies waited with bated breath, knowing that the fate of Everest Corp and The Syndicate rested in the hands of twelve jurors.

Hours turned into days as the jury deliberated, the suspense of their decision a relentless force that hung over them all. Finally, the moment of truth arrived as the jury returned to the courtroom, their faces solemn, their decision reached.

The judge read the verdict, and a collective gasp filled the courtroom. Everest Corp was found guilty of corporate corruption and complicity in The

Syndicate's actions. The suspense in the courtroom gave way to a wave of relief and triumph, as justice was served, and the battle against corporate corruption had achieved a significant victory.

Sarah couldn't help but feel a sense of vindication as she watched Everest Corp's executives led away in handcuffs. The suspense of their investigation had transformed into a relentless quest for justice, and they had prevailed against the forces of corporate power.

As they emerged from the courtroom, victorious but battle-worn, Sarah knew that the fight for corporate accountability was far from over. The suspense of their battle had exposed The Syndicate's secrets and brought Everest Corp to justice, but the shadows of deception and danger still loomed.

Their mission to expose corporate corruption had been a perilous journey, a relentless pursuit of the truth, and it had come at a great cost. But the suspense of their investigation had brought them to a moment of reckoning, a testament to their unwavering commitment to the pursuit of justice.

As they moved forward, they knew that Everest Corp's agents and The Syndicate's enforcers would not rest, that the battle against corporate corruption was an ongoing struggle. But they remained steadfast, knowing that the suspense of their pursuit was a force for change, a determination to hold those in power accountable.

The final chapter of their investigation had been written, but the story of their fight for justice continued. The suspense of their mission would carry them into a future where corporate accountability was no longer a dream but a reality, a testament to the power of relentless determination and the pursuit of truth.

www.ingramcontent.com/pod-product-compliance
Lightning Source LLC
LaVergne TN
LVHW050027080526
838202LV00069B/6945